It's not somebody who has seen the light
It's a cold and it's a broken Hallelujah

Hallelujah, Hallelujah
Hallelujah, Hallelujah

You say I took the name in vain
I don't even know the name
But if I did, well, really, what's it to you?
There's a blaze of light in every word
It doesn't matter which you heard
The holy or the broken Hallelujah

Hallelujah, Hallelujah
Hallelujah, Hallelujah

I did my best, it wasn't much
I couldn't feel, so I tried to touch
I've told the truth, I didn't come to fool you
And even though it all went wrong
I'll stand before the Lord of Song
With nothing on my tongue but Hallelujah

Hallelujah, Hallelujah
Hallelujah, Hallelujah
Hallelujah, Hallelujah
Hallelujah, Hallelujah
Hallelujah, Hallelujah
Hallelujah, Hallelujah
Hallelujah, Hallelujah
Hallelujah, Hallelujah
Hallelujah

PIANO · VOCAL · GUITAR

# CHART HITS
## OF 2017-2018

ISBN 978-1-5400-2323-0

HAL•LEONARD®

7777 W. BLUEMOUND RD. P.O. BOX 13819 MILWAUKEE, WI 53213

Visit Hal Leonard Online at
**www.halleonard.com**

# ATTENTION

Words and Music by CHARLIE PUTH
and JACOB HINDLIN

Moderate Pop groove

Whoa. _____    Mmm. ____

You've been    run-nin' 'round, run-nin' 'round, run-nin' 'round, throw-in' that

dirt    all    on    my    name    'cause you    knew    that I,    knew that I,    knew that I'd    call    you

*Recorded a half step higher.*

# FEEL IT STILL

Words and Music by JOHN GOURLEY,
ZACH CAROTHERS, JASON SECHRIST,
ERIC HOWK, KYLE O'QUIN, BRIAN HOLLAND,
FREDDIE GORMAN, GEORGIA DOBBINS,
ROBERT BATEMAN, WILLIAM GARRETT,
JOHN HILL and ASA TACCONE

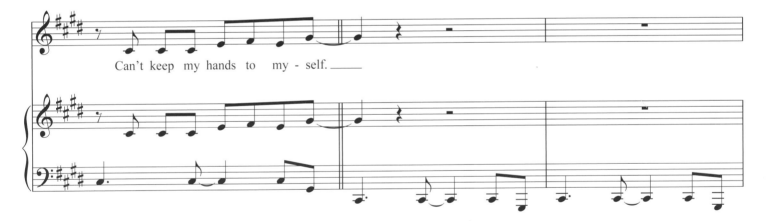

Can't keep my hands to my - self. ____

Think I'll dust 'em off, put 'em back up on the shelf, ____ case my

# END GAME

Words and Music by TAYLOR SWIFT,
ED SHEERAN, MAX MARTIN, SHELLBACK
and NAYVADIUS WILBURN

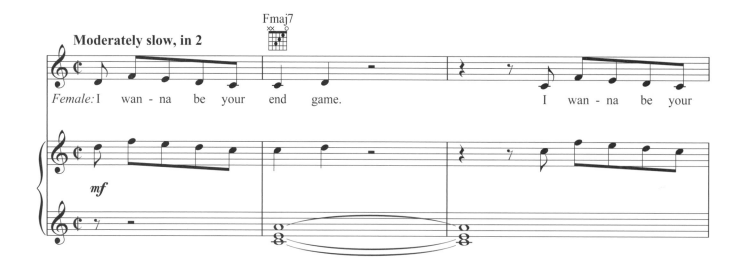

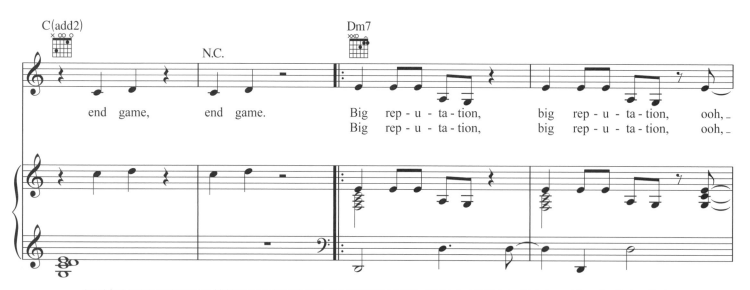

# GREATEST LOVE STORY

Words and Music by
BRANDON LANCASTER

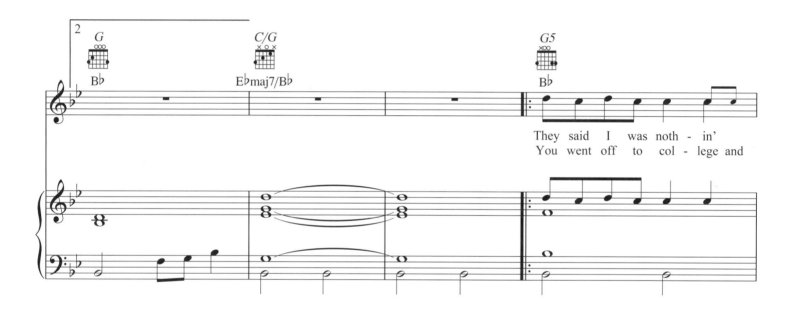

They said I was noth-in'
You went off to col-lege and

but a trou-ble-mak-er and nev-er up to no good. ___
I ___ got a job. I was work-in' that nine to five. ___

# HAVANA

Words and Music by CAMILA CABELLO, LOUIS BELL,
PHARRELL WILLIAMS, ADAM FEENEY, ALI TAMPOSI,
BRIAN LEE, ANDREW WOTMAN, BRITTANY HAZZARD,
JEFFERY LAMAR WILLIAMS and BRANDON PERRY

*Additional Lyrics*

Jeffery.
Just graduated, fresh on campus, mmm.
Fresh out East Atlanta with no manners, damn.
Fresh out East Atlanta.
Bump on her bumper like a traffic jam (jam).
Hey, I was quick to pay that girl like Uncle Sam. (Here you go, ay).
Back it on me, shawty cravin' on me.
Get to diggin' on me (on me).
She waited on me. (Then what?)
Shawty cakin' on me, got the bacon on me. (Wait up.)
This is history in the makin' on me (on me).
Point blank, close range, that be.
If it cost a million, that's me (that's me).
I was gettin' mula, man, they feel me.

# ISSUES

Words and Music by BENJAMIN LEVIN,
MIKKEL ERIKSEN, TOR HERMANSEN,
JULIA MICHAELS and JUSTIN TRANTER

# LIABILITY

Words and Music by ELLA YELICH-O'CONNOR
and JACK ANTONOFF

* Recorded a half step lower.
** Vocal written one octave higher than sung.

# LOCATION

Words and Music by KHALID ROBINSON,
JOSHUA SCRUGGS, SAMUEL JIMENEZ,
CHRIS McCLENNEY, OLATUNJI IGE,
ALFREDO GONZALEZ and BARJAM KURTI

(Sung:) Oh,

I don't need __ noth-in' else ___ but you.

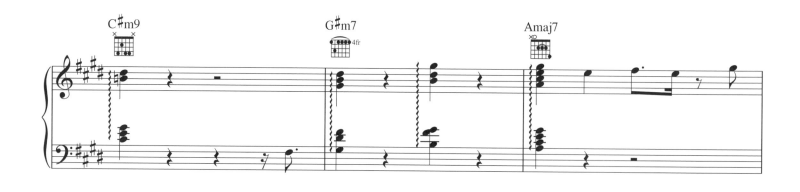

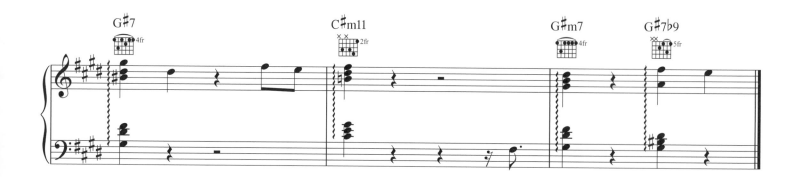

# LUST FOR LIFE

Words and Music by ELIZABETH GRANT,
RICK NOWELS, MAX MARTIN
and ABEL TESFAYE

# PERFECT

Words and Music by
ED SHEERAN

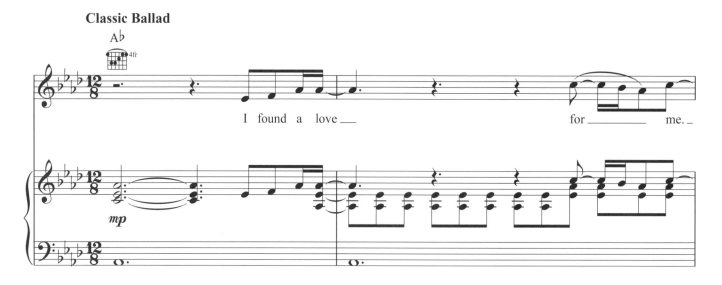

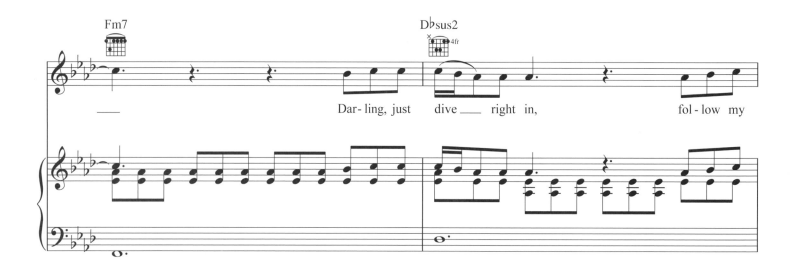

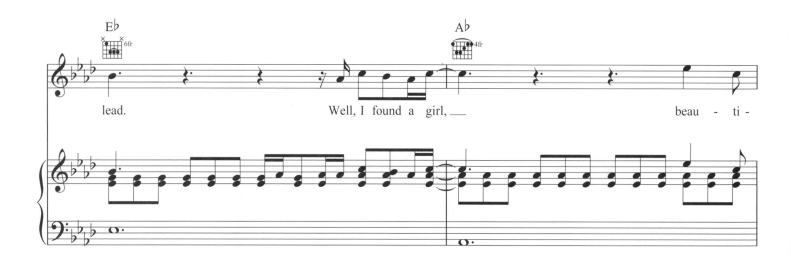

# PRAYING

Words and Music by KESHA SEBERT,
BEN ABRAHAM, RYAN LEWIS
and ANDREW JOSLYN

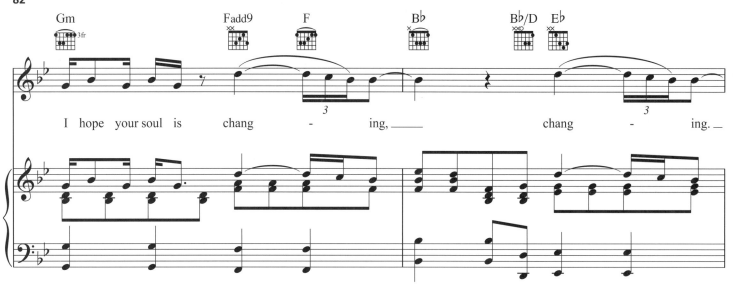

I hope your soul is chang - ing,_____ chang - ing.__

___ I hope you find your peace_____ fall - ing on ___ your knees, _

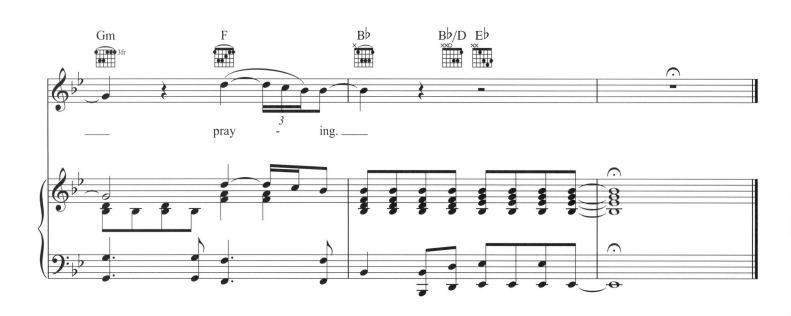

___ pray - ing. ____

# REDBONE

Words and Music by DONALD GLOVER,
LUDWIG GORANSSON, GEORGE CLINTON,
WILLIAM COLLINS and GARY COOPER

**Moderately slow groove**

\* *Recorded a half step higher.*

close  your  eyes. _____

(Lead vocal ad lib.)

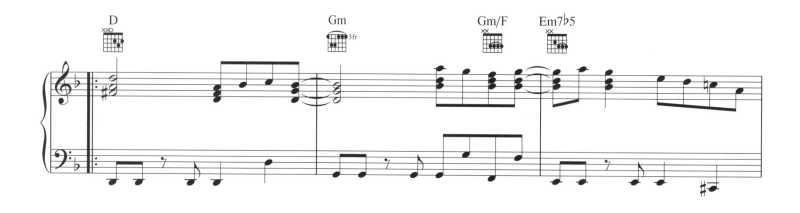

Play 3 times

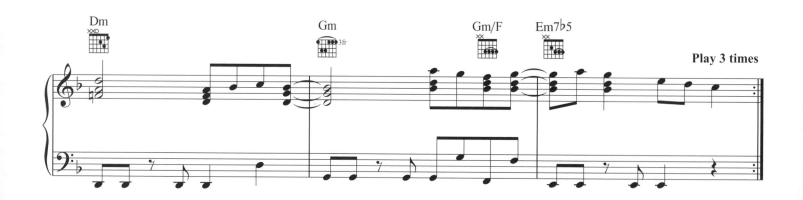

But stay woke.

But stay woke.

# SORRY NOT SORRY

Words and Music by DEMITRIA LOVATO,
SEAN DOUGLAS, WARREN FELDER,
WILLIAM SIMMONS and TREVOR BROWN

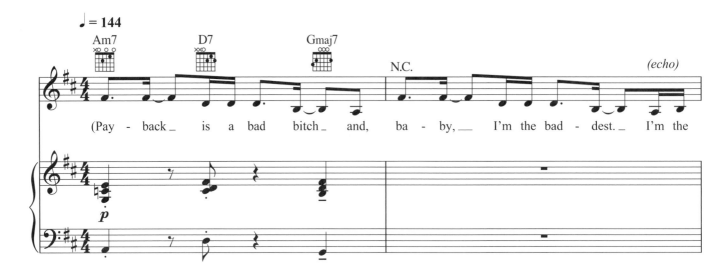

# THERE'S NOTHING HOLDIN' ME BACK

Words and Music by SHAWN MENDES,
GEOFFREY WARBURTON, TEDDY GEIGER
and SCOTT HARRIS

**Acoustic Pop**

I wan - na fol - low where she goes,
She says that she's nev - er a - fraid;

I think a - bout her and she knows it. ___
just pic - ture ev - 'ry - bod - y na - ked. ___

I wan - na let her take con -
She real - ly does - n't like to

trol;
wait,

'cause ev - 'ry time that she gets clos - er, she
not real - ly in - to hes - i - ta - tion.

# THUNDER

Words and Music by DAN REYNOLDS,
WAYNE SERMON, BEN McKEE,
DANIEL PLATZMAN, ALEXANDER GRANT
and JAYSON DeZUZIO

**Steady Rock**

Just a young gun with a quick fuse, I was up-tight, want to let loose.

I was dream-ing of big-ger things and want to leave my own life be-hind.

Not a yes sir, not a fol-low-er. Fit the box, fit the mold, have a seat in the

# TOO GOOD AT GOODBYES

Words and Music by SAM SMITH,
TOR HERMANSEN, MIKKEL ERIKSEN
and JAMES NAPIER

**Pop Ballad**

You must think that I'm stu - pid. You must think that I'm a

fool.\_\_\_\_ You must think that I'm new \_\_ to this, \_\_

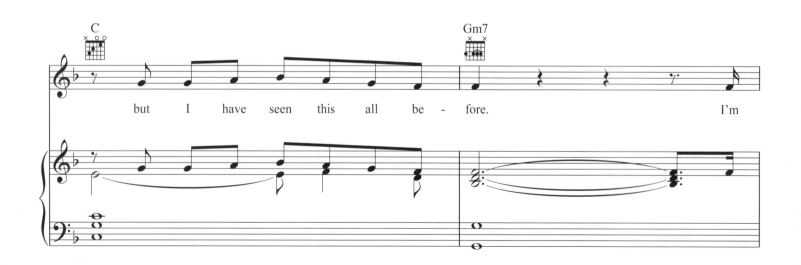

but I have seen this all be - fore. I'm

# WHAT ABOUT US

Words and Music by ALECIA MOORE,
STEVE MAC and JOHNNY McDAID

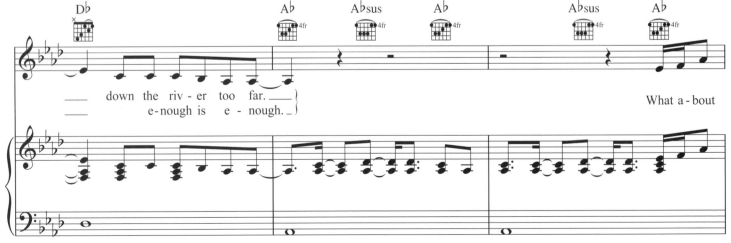

118

# WHAT LOVERS DO

Words and Music by ADAM LEVINE,
SOLANA ROWE, JASON EVIGAN,
OLADAYO OLATUNJI, BRITTANY HAZZARD,
VICTOR RAADSTROM and BEN DIEHL

# THE NEW DECADE SERIES

## Books with Online Audio • Arranged for Piano, Voice, and Guitar

The New Decade Series features collections of iconic songs from each decade with great backing tracks so you can play them and sound like a pro. You access the tracks online for streaming or download. **See complete song listings online at www.halleonard.com**

## SONGS OF THE 1920s
Ain't Misbehavin' • Baby Face • California, Here I Come • Fascinating Rhythm • I Wanna Be Loved by You • It Had to Be You • Mack the Knife • Ol' Man River • Puttin' on the Ritz • Rhapsody in Blue • Someone to Watch over Me • Tea for Two • Who's Sorry Now • and more.
00137576 P/V/G..................................$24.99

## SONGS OF THE 1930s
As Time Goes By • Blue Moon • Cheek to Cheek • Embraceable You • A Fine Romance • Georgia on My Mind • I Only Have Eyes for You • The Lady Is a Tramp • On the Sunny Side of the Street • Over the Rainbow • Pennies from Heaven • Stormy Weather (Keeps Rainin' All the Time) • The Way You Look Tonight • and more.
00137579 P/V/G..................................$24.99

## SONGS OF THE 1940s
At Last • Boogie Woogie Bugle Boy • Don't Get Around Much Anymore • God Bless' the Child • How High the Moon • It Could Happen to You • La Vie En Rose (Take Me to Your Heart Again) • Route 66 • Sentimental Journey • The Trolley Song • You'd Be So Nice to Come Home To • Zip-A-Dee-Doo-Dah • and more.
00137582 P/V/G..................................$24.99

## SONGS OF THE 1950s
Ain't That a Shame • Be-Bop-A-Lula • Chantilly Lace • Earth Angel • Fever • Great Balls of Fire • Love Me Tender • Mona Lisa • Peggy Sue • Que Sera, Sera (Whatever Will Be, Will Be) • Rock Around the Clock • Sixteen Tons • A Teenager in Love • That'll Be the Day • Unchained Melody • Volare • You Send Me • Your Cheatin' Heart • and more.
00137595 P/V/G..................................$24.99

## SONGS OF THE 1960s
All You Need Is Love • Beyond the Sea • Born to Be Wild • California Girls • Dancing in the Street • Happy Together • King of the Road • Leaving on a Jet Plane • Louie, Louie • My Generation • Oh, Pretty Woman • Sunshine of Your Love • Under the Boardwalk • You Really Got Me • and more.
00137596 P/V/G ..................................$24.99

## SONGS OF THE 1970s
ABC • Bridge over Troubled Water • Cat's in the Cradle • Dancing Queen • Free Bird • Goodbye Yellow Brick Road • Hotel California • I Will Survive • Joy to the World • Killing Me Softly with His Song • Layla • Let It Be • Piano Man • The Rainbow Connection • Stairway to Heaven • The Way We Were • Your Song • and more.
00137599 P/V/G ..................................$27.99

## SONGS OF THE 1980s
Addicted to Love • Beat It • Careless Whisper • Come on Eileen • Don't Stop Believin' • Every Rose Has Its Thorn • Footloose • I Just Called to Say I Love You • Jessie's Girl • Livin' on a Prayer • Saving All My Love for You • Take on Me • Up Where We Belong • The Wind Beneath My Wings • and more.
00137600 P/V/G ..................................$27.99

## SONGS OF THE 1990s
Angel • Black Velvet • Can You Feel the Love Tonight • (Everything I Do) I Do It for You • Friends in Low Places • Hero • I Will Always Love You • More Than Words • My Heart Will Go On (Love Theme from 'Titanic') • Smells like Teen Spirit • Under the Bridge • Vision of Love • Wonderwall • and more.
00137601 P/V/G ..................................$27.99

## SONGS OF THE 2000s
Bad Day • Beautiful • Before He Cheats • Chasing Cars • Chasing Pavements • Drops of Jupiter (Tell Me) • Fireflies • Hey There Delilah • How to Save a Life • I Gotta Feeling • I'm Yours • Just Dance • Love Story • 100 Years • Rehab • Unwritten • You Raise Me Up • and more.
00137608 P/V/G..............................$27.99

## SONGS OF THE 2010s
All About That Bass • All of Me • Brave • Empire State of Mind • Get Lucky • Happy • Hey, Soul Sister • I Knew You Were Trouble • Just the Way You Are • Need You Now • Pompeii • Radioactive • Rolling in the Deep • Shake It Off • Shut up and Dance • Stay with Me • Take Me to Church • Thinking Out Loud • Uptown Funk • and many more.
00151836 P/V/G ..................................$27.99

## HAL•LEONARD®

**halleonard.com**
Prices, content, and availability
subject to change without notice.

0317